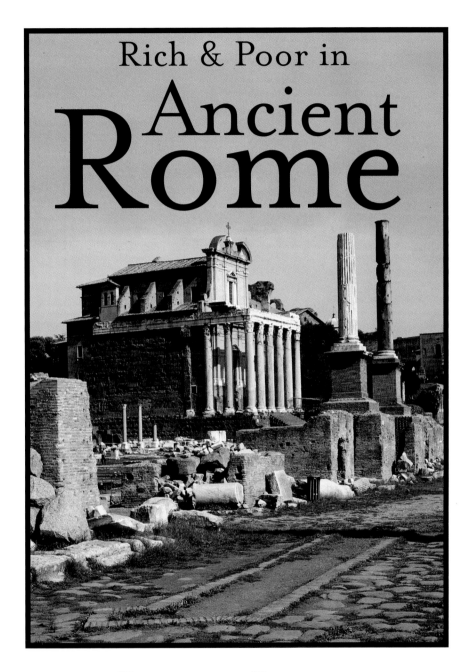

Rich & Poor in
Ancient
Rome

RICHARD DARGIE

W
FRANKLIN WATTS
LONDON • SYDNEY

First published in 2005 by
Franklin Watts
96 Leonard Street
London EC2A 4XD

Franklin Watts Australia
Level 17/207 Kent Street
Sydney
NSW 2000

Produced by Arcturus Publishing Ltd,
26/27 Bickels Yard, 151-153 Bermondsey Street, London SE1 3HA

Series concept: Alex Woolf
Editor: Alex Woolf
Designer: Tim Mayer
Illustrator: Adam Hook
Picture researcher: Glass Onion Pictures

Picture Credits:
Art Archive: 4 (Rheinischeslandesmuseum Bonn / Dagli Orti), 6 (Dagli Orti),
7 (Museo della Civilta Romana, Rome / Dagli Orti), 8 (Dagli Orti), 10
(Egyptian Museum, Cairo / Dagli Orti), 12 (Archaeological Museum, Naples /
Dagli Orti), 13 (Archaeological Museum, Naples / Dagli Orti [A]), 14
(Archaeological Museum, Naples / Dagli Orti [A]), 15 (Museo della Civilta
Romana, Rome / Dagli Orti), 19 (Museo della Civilta Romana, Rome / Dagli
Orti), 20 (Dagli Orti), 21 (Museo Nazionale Terme, Rome / Dagli Orti), 22
(Bardo Museum, Tunis / Dagli Orti), 23 (Museo della Civilta Romana, Rome /
Dagli Orti), 25 (National Museum, Bucharest / Dagli Orti), front cover and
26 (Dagli Orti), 27 (Archaeological Museum, Naples / Dagli Orti), 28
(Provinciaal Museum G M Kam Nijmegen, Netherlands / Dagli Orti).
Bridgeman Art Library: 16 (Rheinisches Landesmuseum, Trier, Germany).

Every attempt has been made to clear copyright. Should there be any
inadvertent omission, please apply to the publisher for rectification.

A CIP catalogue record for this book is available from the British Library.

ISBN 07496 5952 1

Printed in Singapore

·CONTENTS·

Rulers of Rome

From 100 BCE to 400 CE, Rome was the richest and most important city in the ancient world. It was the capital of an empire that stretched across Europe from Britain to North Africa and the Middle East. Great wealth poured into the city and much of it was enjoyed by the noble families who ruled the city.

This first-century tomb carving shows a Roman knight, with his richly decorated horse, the symbol of his wealth and power.

✖ SENATORS AND KNIGHTS ✖

The richest Roman nobles belonged to the senator class. They sat in the senate, the assembly of six hundred men that passed laws and ran the government of Rome. The next rank of Romans were the equestrians, or knights, who were often rich from trade and banking but who also held government posts.

UNSUITABLE JOBS

Romans from well-born families could not follow occupations that were considered vulgar, as the writer Cicero explained: "Trades involving manual labour are unsuitable for a gentleman.... More respectable trades are those which need intelligence such as medicine, architecture and teaching. But of all the occupations none is more suitable than owning a farm."

From the letters of Marcus Tullius Cicero

The Roman Poor

Romans who were not noble or knights were called plebeians. Although poor, many plebeians were full Roman citizens. In early Roman times, they were able to vote for their leaders. Under the emperors, these free citizens still had many privileges. They had the right to wear the toga and the right to free food from the government. Only citizens were allowed to fight in the Roman legions.

❧ Slaves ❧

Many of the poorer people who lived in Rome were slaves. Some slaves were prisoners taken in wars, while others were kidnapped for the slave markets, or were the children of slaves.

Life was hard for many slaves. Those who worked in chain gangs in the silver mines or in the crop fields of Italy were soon worn out and died. Others had more pleasant lives working as servants in the houses of the rich. Intelligent slaves, often from Greece, sometimes rose to become doctors, teachers or artists.

Domestic slaves had busy lives serving their masters and were expected to work as waiters and cleaners around the house.

A Desirable Domus

This first-century wall painting from the town of Pompeii shows the villa of a wealthy Roman family. Many villas had colonnades offering shelter from the hot summer sun.

Most wealthy Romans lived in a free-standing house called a *domus*. This was usually built of brick or cut stone with a red-tile roof. The rooms were arranged in a square around an open courtyard. The domus was cool in summer because the windows were shaded from the sun by wooden shutters. Underfloor heating and iron braziers burning charcoal kept the domus warm during the short Italian winter.

❋ LUXURY AND SECURITY ❋

The wealthy could also afford to employ skilled craftsmen, costing over a hundred denarii (about £500 in today's money) a day, to decorate their walls with paintings and their floors with mosaics. To prevent burglars gaining access, there were no windows on the ouside walls of a domus. At night, the *atriensis* — a trusted slave responsible for security — slept by the heavy, bolted main door of the house.

A Plebeian's Place

Almost a million people lived in Rome in 100 CE, and there was not enough space for everyone to live in a domus. Most poorer Romans – and even some who were not so poor – lived in flats in tenement buildings called *insulae*, or islands. These insulae were often quite small and poorly built, but since many people wanted to live in Rome, they could cost as much as 30,000 sesterces (about £40,000) a year to rent.

⊰ CRAMPED CONDITIONS ⊱

The poorer buildings usually had no lavatories or running water. Tenants had to bring their water up from the public fountains in the street and use the public latrines. They cooked their meals in cramped kitchens, using wood or charcoal on small stoves. The insulae were also built very close together. As a result fire and disease could spread easily from one building to another.

In the poorer districts of ancient Rome, the insulae were tightly packed together. The buildings were often several storeys high because land for building was scarce and expensive.

LANDLORD'S COMPLAINT

The writer Cicero was unhappy about an insula he had bought to rent out: "Two of the ground-floor shops in my insula have collapsed and the walls of the other rooms have cracked badly. My tenants have all left – and so have the mice !"

From the letters of Marcus Tullius Cicero

The Nobles at Home

In rich Roman families, fathers had great control over the other members of the family. Even a middle-aged man had to obey the decisions of his elderly father. Women had very few rights.

Noble men and women were married in a religious ceremony during which they exchanged wafers of wheat in front of the temple priests. Marriages between noble families were serious affairs because money and land were also involved.

The Roman imperial family wore the traditional toga to show that they were members of old, noble clans.

❖ EDUCATION ❖

Rich children were taught to read and write by Greek slaves called tutors. Most noble boys were trained in the skills of a soldier. When they were older, they were taught about the law and government. Girls were trained in making a home and bringing up children.

THE IDEAL WIFE

Roman wives were expected to be loyal and brave. The writer Pliny described Arria, the ideal Roman wife. Her husband Paetus, sentenced to death for plotting against the emperor, was allowed the privilege of committing suicide. When he hesitated to use his dagger, Arria plunged it into her own chest, then handed it back to Paetus saying, "Look husband, it doesn't hurt at all."

Letter from Pliny the Younger to Nepos

Plebeian Families

In early Roman times, poorer Roman men sometimes bought a wife from her family. After giving a gift to the bride's father, the groom carried his new wife over the threshold of his house. In imperial times, plebeian men and women were considered to be married if they lived together for a year.

❧ ABANDONED CHILDREN ❧

Very few children from poorer families learned to read or write. Instead, most poorer children learned a trade by working alongside their parents.

Once plebeian parents had enough children to carry on the family name and business, new infants were often abandoned.

They were extra mouths who would be expensive to feed and clothe. These infants died of starvation or were collected by slave traders who sold them in the markets. In the second century CE, the emperor Trajan built orphanages for these poor children, and the empress Faustina built schools where abandoned girls were given an education.

A Roman craftsman teaches his son how to produce a mosaic. Poorer children learned the skills they would need for their working lives in the workshop rather than the schoolroom.

Forum Fashions

Wealthy Roman citizens wore the toga, a sheet of fine wool or linen draped around the body. Most wore a plain white toga, but senators' togas were edged with purple. Over the toga, a nobleman wore a cloak of fine wool from Asia Minor. Rich Roman women wore a pleated gown called a *stola* which usually reached down to their feet.

After 100 BCE many rich Romans wore a brightly coloured robe called a *synthesis* for evening dinner parties.

✖ FOOTWEAR ✖

Wealthy Romans wore shoes that showed their rank. Nobles wore red sandals, but only consuls (elected governors of Rome) were allowed to wear white shoes. Women wore white or yellow shoes that covered their toes.

TOGAS

Only Roman citizens were allowed to wear the toga. Slaves and foreigners visiting Rome were punished if they were caught wearing one. The poet Virgil described the Romans as "the Lords of the World, the race that wears the toga". However, togas were expensive and plebeian Romans only possessed one for special occasions.

From Virgil's *Aeneid* Book I

This figurine shows the goddess Isis wearing a long pleated stola, or gown, under a fine woollen palla, or shawl.

Clothes for Commoners

Slaves and most plebeian Romans usually wore tunics which were like long, knee-length tee shirts. In the summer, they wore cool linen tunics, but switched to warmer woollen ones in the winter months. Heating rooms at night was expensive, so poorer Romans often wore several tunics to keep warm in bed.

Over their tunic, most poor Roman men wore a cloak of rough wool. Women wore a simple dress called a *tunica*. When they went out, they also wore a long shawl called a *palla* to cover their shoulders and head.

Workers dressed in a simple cloak made of one piece of leather with a hole cut for the head. Poorer Romans had to walk everywhere, so they wore leather sandals.

◈ BREECHES ◈

In the fourth century, some Romans began wearing *bracae* (breeches), like the Gauls, but the emperor Honorius banned the wearing of these trousers within the city because they were a "barbarian" form of dress.

Some masters dressed their slaves in a special livery, or uniform. The stripes on the tunic of the slave in this third-century mosaic probably show that he belonged to a noble house.

Gourmets and Gluttons

Some wealthy Romans ate a great deal. There were often ten or more main courses to a dinner at a Roman nobleman's house. Guests took salty drinks called emetics to vomit up each course before tasting the next.

One glutton, Apicius, was famous for serving strange dishes such as flamingo tongues, camel heels and stuffed sow's womb at his banquets. He spent his fortune on vast banquets and then committed suicide because he could not face life without eating exotic foods.

Many rich Romans held lavish banquets to show off their wealth. They hired singers and poets to entertain the guests.

❖ DIETING ❖

Many wealthy Romans were overweight. In 164 CE the doctor Galen prescribed a diet of raw vegetables with vinegar for his obese patients and told them to eat chicken instead of fattier meats. The Roman government passed laws to try and stop its citizens from spending too much on banquets. Fancy foods such as dormice and oysters were banned in 115 BCE.

Some wealthy Romans were careful with their diet and their money. The politician Cato only ate uncooked food, as he thought meat was unhealthy and he considered fuel for cooking too expensive.

Meals for the Masses

Many poorer Romans did not make enough money to feed themselves and their families, so the government gave them small tokens called *tesserae*. They could exchange the tesserae for wheat meal at the public granaries. They boiled this in water to make a rough, grey porridge. Many then added mushrooms, herbs, olives and small pieces of fish or meat to give it flavour.

The meat from animals sacrificed in temples was also handed out to the Roman poor. Slaves were given a thick, grey, chewy bread made from barley.

❧ FAST FOOD ❧

Many ordinary Romans bought "fast food" from snack bars in the street. Here they could buy small sausages called *tomaculi*, or pieces of cooked meat covered in a spicy sauce called *garum*, made from fish entrails. Like their richer neighbours, plebeian Romans drank wine mixed with water.

The poorest Romans queued every morning at the public granary to receive their ration of free bread from the government.

SHOPPING LIST

A plebeian from Pompeii bought the following in 79 CE: "on the sixth day of the month, one ass spent on cheese, eight asses on bread, three on oil and three on wine."

Graffito from Pompeii

Doctors and Dentists

The wealthiest Romans lived in clean houses, with fresh running water from the city aqueducts. After 100 CE many rich citizens had water closets and heated baths in their homes.

If they were ill, they could afford to call in one of the Greek doctors who practised in the city. Diseases such as malaria were rife during the autumn fever season, but the rich could escape to their homes in the countryside. Many went to spa towns such as Clancianum that had healing thermal waters.

✖ FALSE TEETH ✖

Wealthy Romans could also afford to replace their rotting teeth with false teeth shaped from ivory or bone. The dentist Archigenes sold an expensive ointment made of roasted earthworms mixed with the eggs of spiders as a treatment for tooth decay.

A surgeon attends a wounded soldier. The Romans studied the workings of the body, and could perform a number of operations.

BEAUTY TIP

The poet Ovid advised poorer girls who could not afford expensive dental care: "If your teeth are blackened or too large or have been squint from birth, laughing aloud is a big mistake; instead learn to laugh quietly and cover your teeth with your lips as you do, and you will be thought beautiful."

From Ovid's *Ars Amatoria*

Danger and Disease

Tombstones tell us that many poor Romans died in their thirties and forties. Most were worn out by their daily work. There were no machines in ancient times and hard jobs had to be done by hand. Many workers and slaves must have suffered from strained heart muscles as a result.

The fullers who worked in laundries died young from breathing fumes from the burning sulphur and urine used in bleaching and cleaning cloth.

◈ IN THE CITY ◈

Many of the poor in Rome lived near the River Tiber, which was full of sewage and rotting food refuse. Romans often fell ill from eating food that had been contaminated by flies. In the hot summer months, lethal diseases such as as typhus, typhoid and malaria were also very common.

Entry to the public baths was very cheap to encourage ordinary Romans to keep themselves clean. During the summer, plebeians were offered free entry to the baths.

Romans who could not afford a doctor often went to their local pharmacy instead, where they could buy remedies made from herbs and minerals.

Ladies of Leisure

This second-century carving shows a rich Roman lady being attended by four young slaves.

Roman women had to obey their menfolk at all times. Even noblewomen had few rights and were not allowed to vote or get divorced. Girls from noble families were often engaged when they were very young. Sometimes they were sent to live with the family of their future husband. In imperial times, women were not even allowed to sit by their husbands at the theatre, but had to sit in seats set aside for women only.

Most wealthy Roman women busied themselves with running their household. The morning began by sending slaves to the market to buy food or to the laundry with soiled linen.

◈ BATHING AND BEAUTY ◈

Later in the morning the mistress would go to the public baths. After bathing, slaves would rub the mistress with pumice stones to remove body hair and dead skin. Slaves plucked the lady's eyebrows and then tied up her hair using the purple ribbons that only noblewomen were allowed to wear. Wealthy women covered their faces at night with a cream made from flour and milk, and used scented pastilles to sweeten their breath.

Working Wives

Some plebeian women were skilled and well paid. Successful midwives were respected and could charge high fees, as could some famous singers and musicians. Many women ran their own businesses as keepers of inns and shops. Most helped their husband or made a modest living spinning and weaving wool, or as washerwomen.

The very poorest women sold themselves into slavery. Female slaves had no legal rights. If they had children, their master could take the children and sell them in the slave market.

✎ MAKE-UP ✎

All Roman women used make-up, but plebeian women could only afford to buy cheaper potions that were very often poor quality. The poet Martial described two such poor women: "Fabella has her face smeared with chalk and fears the rain, while Sabella is covered with red face-cream and fears the sun."

Some poor Roman women became gladiators and tried to win a fortune by fighting in the arena.

EPITAPH

A tombstone inscription remembers "Amymone, wife of Marcus, who lies here, and was a most good wife, a most beautiful woman, obedient, careful, a gifted spinner of wool who built a good home."

Sepulchral inscription, Rome

Patrons and Lawyers

A Roman noble's day began with the *salutatio*. He would go to the main entrance of his house and meet his clients. They were poorer people who depended on him for a living or for favours. The clients would flatter their noble patron and in return they received a gift of money or a small basket of food called a *sportula*. If the noble stood in an election, he expected his clients to vote for him.

After the salutatio, most nobles went to the law courts at the forum, the city's public meeting place. Many nobles were lawyers. They spent their mornings arguing in court or dictating letters to their scribes. Important politicians might give a speech in the senate. Many noble Romans also worked as bankers, lending money to traders and collecting taxes for the government.

※ BUSY LIVES ※

The writer and lawyer Pliny complained that his days were too busy: "This morning alone I witnessed a coming-of-age ceremony, attended a wedding engagement, witnessed a will for a client, supported another client in the law courts and gave legal advice to yet another."

Roman officials depended heavily on their scribes. Scribes were well-educated slaves who were skilled in copying letters and storing business records.

Another Day, Another Denarius

Small traders like this butcher joined societies or clubs. These looked after their members in times of hardship and paid a small pension to their widows.

Many poorer Romans had no job and they depended on gifts like the sportula from their patron. Others had small businesses as craftsmen or shopkeepers. A skilled craftsman such as a painter and decorator could make as much as 150 denarii (about £750) per day, while a tailor would charge sixty denarii (about £300) for making a hooded cloak.

❧ LOW WAGES ❧

However, unskilled labourers struggled to make a living. The men who cleaned out the Cloaca Maxima, Rome's underground sewer, were paid just four denarii (about £20) per day. The very poorest Romans could sell themselves into slavery.

PUBLIC MONEY

During periods of economic slump, the emperor used public money to build bridges, fountains or monuments, giving jobs to unemployed citizens. When an engineer showed the emperor Vespasian his plans for a mechanical way of moving heavy objects without using many workers, the emperor ordered him away, saying: "You must allow me to feed my poor common people."

From *The Life of Vespasian* by Gaius Suetonius Tranquillus

A Grand Day Out

All Romans liked to watch chariot races and the gladiatorial games. After 80 CE the best place to watch gladiators was the Flavian Amphitheatre, now known as the Colosseum. Noble Romans often paid for the games and chariot races. They did this to win favour with the ordinary citizens, hoping that they would support them in elections for important jobs in the government.

❖ BEST SEATS IN THE HOUSE ❖

The most important Romans sat in the front row of seats, nearest to the arena. The emperor sat with his favourites on the imperial podium. Senators had a special balcony called the *pulvinar*, close to the emperor. The next tier of seats was reserved for knights from the equestrian class. Members of the richest noble families had their own reserved marble chairs.

The Colosseum was used for gladiatorial combats. It could comfortably seat crowds of up to 60,000 spectators.

Amusing the Masses

This second-century fresco shows Roman plebians playing with a ball. The government encouraged men to stay fit so that they would be useful in wartime.

Ordinary Roman citizens had a lot of free time. Slaves did many jobs and so most citizens only had to work six hours each day. Every eighth day, the *nundina*, was a public holiday. On the nundina, some poorer Romans exercised on the Field of Mars, a large open space where many Romans went to wrestle or play with balls. Many went to the games to spectate and gamble.

❧ PECKING ORDER ❧

Although entry to the Colosseum was free, poor Romans were only allowed to sit in the highest sections of the stadium, behind the senators and knights. Even here there was a strict hierarchy. Soldiers were given the best seats, then married men. The seats with the poorest view of the action were left for women and slaves.

BREAD AND CIRCUSES

The Roman writer Marcus Cornelius Fronto (95–170 CE) explained why the gladiatorial games were so important in ancient Rome: "A wise emperor knows that the Roman people are kept loyal by a supply of free grain and by the games…. Giving out money and grain keeps the plebs content while the races and games keep the whole population happy."

From the letters of Marcus Cornelius Fronto

Holiday Homes

The richest Roman citizens owned large farm estates in the countryside called latifundia. These landowners usually left Rome during the summer months and went to live on their estates, avoiding the smells and diseases of the hot, crowded city.

This mosaic from the fourth century CE shows a luxurious villa on an estate in North Africa.

✕ WORK AND LEISURE ✕

Some estate owners took an interest in their farms. Others, like the writer Pliny, went to their country estates to get on with other kinds of work like writing. Many rich Romans just used their estates as holiday homes where they could relax and take part in country sports like hunting. At the centre of the farm estate was the owner's villa, a large, cool mansion where he lived with his family.

Working on a Farm Estate

This stone carving shows a Roman goatherd collecting milk from his flock.

The farm estate was run by an experienced slave called a *vilicus*, or steward. While the master was away, the vilicus was in charge of everything on the estate, including the slaves that worked on the farm.

The life of most farm slaves was very hard. If an estate owner was attacked by one of his slaves, he had the right to crucify all the others. Trusted slaves were allowed to live on the latifundia unchained, and were given their own small room in a block of barracks. Most, however, were kept in iron fetters, even when working in the fields, and slept in underground prisons at night.

⚜ COSTLY SLAVES ⚜

In later Roman times, skilled slaves became very expensive to buy and keep. In 300 CE, a slave who knew how to tend vines could cost up to four thousand denarii (about £20,000) in the slave markets. It became cheaper to hire free men to do jobs on the farms and, in time, fewer farms used slaves as labourers.

Soldiers of Fortune

The most important officers in the Roman army were senators and knights. Each legion or regiment in the army was commanded by a general called a *legatus*. He was a senator and wore a white and purple cape. He was helped by six officers called tribunes who were also from noble families.

◈ A ROUTE TO POWER ◈

Young Romans from wealthy families usually spent three years as army officers. They had to do this if they wanted to become politicians and enter the senate. Some tribunes stayed in the army and made a career as a soldier. They hoped to win fame in battle and be rewarded with lands and honours from the government.

VICTORY PARADE

The writer Flavius Josephus described the victory parade of the emperor Vespasian: "All the legion marched through Rome in companies and by rank behind their commanders. Vespasian emerged, crowned in laurel and dressed in a toga of ancient purple, and led his men to the place where the senators were waiting in their chairs of ivory. The troops shouted with joy and acclaimed Vespasian's bravery."

From *The Jewish War* by Flavius Josephus

Roman army officers wore a one-piece breastplate of silver or bronze. Their rank was probably shown by the coloured trim of their cloak.

Life in the Legion

Poorer Roman citizens usually served in the army as a legionary, or ordinary foot soldier. Legionaries usually lived in barracks when they were on duty. In the barracks, about twenty men shared a living and cooking space with the other members of their unit.

Some of their wages were deducted to pay for their food, uniform and weapons. If they won booty, half of it was saved for the men by the legion in its treasury. This ensured that even the poorest soldier had some savings to fall back on in later life.

If legionaries survived twenty-five years in the army, they retired to a *colonia*. This was a small town where soldiers were given a house, some farmland and a small pension.

◈ CENTURIONS ◈

The best soldiers could become centurions or junior officers in charge of eighty to a hundred men. Centurions were skilled and experienced soldiers and so their annual pay was much higher.

This stone carving from Trajan's Column in Rome shows legionaries hard at work building a fortified camp while on campaign.

Ceremony and Sacrifice

Romans of all classes believed in many gods. Among the most important were Ceres, the goddess of the earth and good harvests, and Vesta, the goddess of the home. Roman soldiers prayed to Mars, the god of war.

The Romans took great care to perform their holy ceremonies in the traditional way. If a mistake was made in their rituals, great misfortune could befall the city. As a result, only men from noble families were trusted to train as priests.

❖ SACRED MYSTERIES ❖

The priests carried out mysterious chants and ceremonies in the ninety temples of Rome. The nobles performed sacrifices of sacred animals, such as oxen, on public altars outside the temples. The common people watched these ceremonies but took no part in them.

Only nobles were allowed to join the college of augurs. These priests told the future by watching for signs from the gods in the weather or in the actions of holy birds.

Many of the most important temples in Rome were in the main Forum. Here, thousands watched the sacrifices and ceremonies that honoured the gods.

Foreign Faiths

All Romans worshipped their ancestors. Even the poorest Roman home had a small shrine called the *lararium* where the family spirit was revered. Every day began with a prayer and a gift of food to the family spirit.

After 70 BCE, growing numbers of poor Romans secretly worshipped a mysterious Persian God called Mithras in underground chapels. They believed that Mithras was the friend of slaves and the poor and would help them to enter heaven after death.

❧ CHRISTIANITY ❧

From 60 CE a new religion, Christianity, spread among the poorer people of Rome. Many poorer Romans became Christians because it offered them the hope of a better life after death.

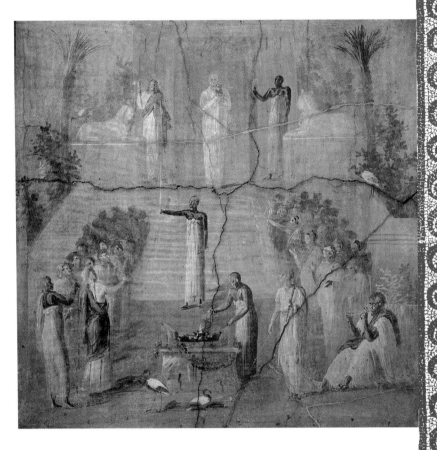

This Roman fresco shows the worship of the Egyptian goddess, Isis. Many poor people in Rome also worshipped gods from other parts of the empire.

ACT OF WORSHIP

Each spring, Romans prayed to the gods for good weather during the planting and growing season. The writer Cato described this important ceremony: "Offer Jupiter a feast of roasted meat and an urn of wine, and honour him with prayers. After the offering, plant garlic, millet and lentils in the fields. Make sure that everyone and everything, even the oxen and their drivers, observes the day as a holiday."

From *On Agriculture* by Marcus Porcius Cato the Elder

Grieving for the Great

The funeral of a Roman noble was a grand affair. First a death mask was made by shaping wax around the face of the corpse. Then the corpse was dressed in its finest toga and placed in a chair or in a litter. The bones of the corpse were broken so that the body could be displayed in a reclining or sitting position as if the noble were still alive.

✷ PROCESSION TO THE FORUM ✷

Slaves carried the chair to the forum, followed by paid mourners who sang sad funeral hymns. The procession took a winding route through the city streets so everyone could see that a great man had died. At the forum, the eldest son gave a speech. Rich Romans were usually cremated and their ashes placed in tombs outside the city along the roads that led to Rome.

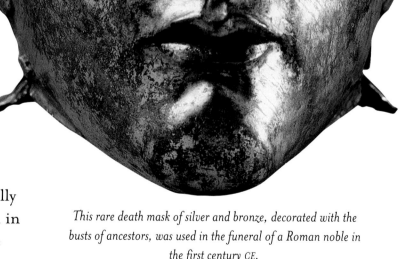

This rare death mask of silver and bronze, decorated with the busts of ancestors, was used in the funeral of a Roman noble in the first century CE.

Budget Burials

When someone from an *insula* died, a cypress branch was placed at the door to tell neighbours that there had been a death. Messengers were sent to relatives to ask for money to help bury the corpse.

The funerals of poor people were simple affairs and were often held at night. Nocturnal funerals were cheaper because there was no need to hire professional mourners or pay for a professional priest. The body was simply accompanied to the place of cremation by relatives and friends.

✤ FUNERAL COLLEGES ✤

Many plebeian Romans belonged to clubs called funeral colleges. They paid a small monthly fee, and when they died their ashes were placed in a niche in a special house for the dead called a columbarium. Slaves were buried with little ceremony in communal pits at the public cemetery on the Esquiline Hill.

REMEMBRANCE

This inscription was written on a tomb in 135 BCE: "Stranger, my message is short so stand there and read it all. Here is the ugly tomb of a lovely woman called Claudia who loved her husband with all her heart. She bore two sons; one lives, the other she placed under the earth. She was charming and gentle and made wool. That's it. Go on your way."

Sepulchral inscription, Rome

Most humble Romans received a simple funeral at night. The torches used in the procession were called funes.

BCE

753 Legendary date of the foundation of the city of Rome.

510 Last king of Rome expelled. Consuls elected as leaders instead.

268 First divorce allowed by Roman law.

264 First gladiatorial show held at Rome.

219 First Greek doctor allowed to practise in the city of Rome.

202 Rome becomes strongest power in the Mediterranean area.

110 The consul Marius organizes the Roman legions properly.

73-71 Revolt of slaves under their leader Spartacus.

27 Augustus becomes first Roman emperor.

CE

64 Hundreds of Roman *insulae*, or tenements, destroyed in the Great Fire.

79 Destruction of Pompeii and Herculaneum by eruption of Vesuvius.

80 Opening of the Flavian Amphitheatre, the Colosseum.

c. 100 Population of city of Rome over one million inhabitants.

180 Roman Empire reaches its greatest size under Emperor Marcus Aurelius.

212 The emperor Caracalla opens vast public baths in Rome.

337 The emperor Constantine becomes a Christian.

391 Worship of the old pagan Roman gods made illegal.

410 Rome captured and sacked by the Visigoths.

476 The last western Roman emperor loses his throne; end of the western Roman Empire.

Further Reading

Look Inside a Roman Villa by Richard Dargie (Wayland, 2002)

Picturing the Past: Ancient Rome by Richard Dargie (Franklin Watts, 2004)

British Museum Activity Books: The Romans by John Reeve and Patricia Vanags (British Museum Press, 1999)

Greek and Roman Fashions by Tom Tierney (Dover Publications, 2001)

Rome: In Spectacular Cross-Section by Andrew Solway and Stephen Biesty (Scholastic, 2003)

Colosseum: Rome's Arena of Death by Peter Connolly (BBC Consumer Publishing, 2003)

Roman Army by Ruth Brocklehurst (Usborne Publishing, 2003)

CD-Roms, Videos, DVDs and Audiocassettes

Ancient Rome: A Journey Back in Time (Cromwell Video Productions, 2000)

Ancient Rome (Castle Home Video, 2001)

The Rotten Romans by Terry Deary (BBC Audiobooks, 2003)

The Romans in North Africa (Cromwell DVD Productions, 2003)

The Romans in Europe (Cromwell DVD Productions, 2003)

The Romans (Arcventure Interactive CD-Rom, 2002)

Explore the Romans, Anglo-Saxons and Vikings (Heinemann CD-Rom, 2002)

Websites

Roman life and times: http://www.bbc.co.uk/schools/romans/

Houses: http://www.roman-empire.net/society/soc-house.html

Family life: http://www.realm-of-shade.com/RomanaeAntiquae/family.html

Clothing: http://www.vroma.org/~bmcmanus/clothing.html

Food: http://www.crystalinks.com/romefood.html

Health: http://www.schoolshistory.org.uk/romanpublichealth.htm

Women: http://www.moyak.com/researcher/resume/papers/roman_women.html

Work: http://depthome.brooklyn.cuny.edu/classics/dunkle/romnlife/rmwrkday.htm

Leisure: http://www.vroma.org/~bmcmanus/leisure.html

Life in the countryside: http://www.historylink101.com/lessons/farm-city/rome1.htm

Army: http://www.roman-empire.net/army/army.html

Religion: http://www.historyforkids.org/learn/romans/religion/

Death and burial: http://museums.ncl.ac.uk/wallnet/sen/Religion.htm

augur A Roman priest who could tell the future and the will of the gods by watching sacred birds.

brazier A raised iron tray for holding hot coals.

breeches Short trousers that reached to just below the knee.

chain gang Slaves chained together and forced to do very hard or dangerous work.

coming-of-age ceremony A family gathering to mark when Roman children were given adult rights.

consul The chief magistrate or law officer in Rome in Republican times.

cremated When a dead body is burned rather than buried.

crucify To execute someone by nailing them to a cross.

denarius (plural: **denarii**) A valuable silver coin used throughout most of the Roman period.

entrails The internal organs of an animal, especially the intestines.

equestrian A horseman or knight and usually a member of the Roman noble class.

forum An open space in a Roman city used for markets and meetings.

fuller A clothmaker who finished and cleaned woollen cloth.

garland A wreath or crown of interwoven flowers or leaves.

gladiator A professional fighter who worked in the Roman arena; originally a swordsman.

glutton A greedy person who eats far too much.

granary A storehouse for grain and other foodstuffs.

insula A tenement building in ancient Rome, usually three or four storeys high.

legion A regiment in the Roman army of between five and six thousand soldiers.

legionary A Roman soldier, usually a foot soldier.

malaria A fever passed on to humans by mosquito bites.

midwife A woman with skill in helping other women to give birth.

niche A small recess or shelf area in a wall.

patron A wealthy man who gives gifts to his friends and supporters.

pleated When cloth is folded over carefully to create a pattern.

plebeian One of the ordinary citizens of Rome.

podium A raised platform that Romans stood on when giving a public speech.

poulterer A trader who sells chickens and other edible birds such as duck.

pumice stone Soft stone made of cooled lava used to remove dead skin.

River Tiber A river that flows through central Italy and Rome to the western Mediterranean.

scribe A secretary or clerk who wrote letters and legal documents for a fee.

senate The main council of Roman government in Republican times.

senator A noble who was a member of the Roman senate.

sestertius (singular of sesterces) A small silver coin worth a fourth of a denarius.

shrine A holy place where images of the gods were placed.

spa town A holiday resort which had healthy spring waters.

squint Not straight.

thermal waters Spring waters heated by natural underground heat.

toga The outer cloak worn by adult Roman citizens.

typhus A dangerous fever caused by the spread of lice in overcrowded housing.

water closet A toilet.

Page numbers in **bold** refer to illustrations.